CATS SET VII

AMERICAN BOBTAIL CATS

Kristin Petrie
ABDO Publishing Company

visit us at
www.abdopublishing.com

Published by ABDO Publishing Company, PO Box 398166, Minneapolis, MN 55439.
Copyright © 2014 by Abdo Consulting Group, Inc. International copyrights reserved
in all countries. No part of this book may be reproduced in any form without written
permission from the publisher. The Checkerboard Library™ is a trademark and logo of
ABDO Publishing Company.

Printed in the United States of America, North Mankato, Minnesota.
052013
112013

PRINTED ON RECYCLED PAPER

Cover Photo: Photo by Helmi Flick
Interior Photos: Glow Images p. 7; Photos by Helmi Flick pp. 5, 9, 11, 13, 15, 16–17,
    19, 21

Editors: Rochelle Baltzer, Megan M. Gunderson
Art Direction: Neil Klinepier

Library of Congress Control Number: 2013932666

Cataloging-in-Publication Data

Petrie, Kristin.
    American bobtail cats / Kristin Petrie.
        p. cm. -- (Cats)
    ISBN 978-1-61783-863-7
    Includes bibliographical references and index.
    1. American bobtail cat--Juvenile literature.   I. Title.
    636.8--dc23

                                                                                    2013932666

CONTENTS

LIONS, TIGERS, AND CATS

What is your favorite animal at the zoo? Is it the monkey? How about the giraffe? Or are you drawn to the sleek, **agile** creatures found in the cat **sanctuary**?

Wild or tame, all cats are from the family **Felidae**. There are more than 30 species in this family. They range from the 400-pound (180-kg) lion to the 7-pound (3-kg) **domestic** house cat.

Domestic cats were **bred** from wild cats thousands of years ago. Back then, humans needed cats to control pests such as mice. Owners eventually realized these cats were also sweet companions. And, they were small enough to live indoors as pets.

Just like their ancestors, today's cats are good hunters.

AMERICAN BOBTAIL CATS

In time, **breeders** noticed that some cats had especially desirable features. They began breeding different types of cats to get the qualities they wanted. So today, there are more than 40 breeds of **domestic** cats.

The American bobtail breed appeared in the late 1960s. While traveling in Arizona, John and Brenda Sanders found a short-tailed brown **tabby** cat.

Back home in Iowa, it mated with their long-tailed cat. The kittens had short tails! Breeders worked with these bobtail kittens to create the American bobtail.

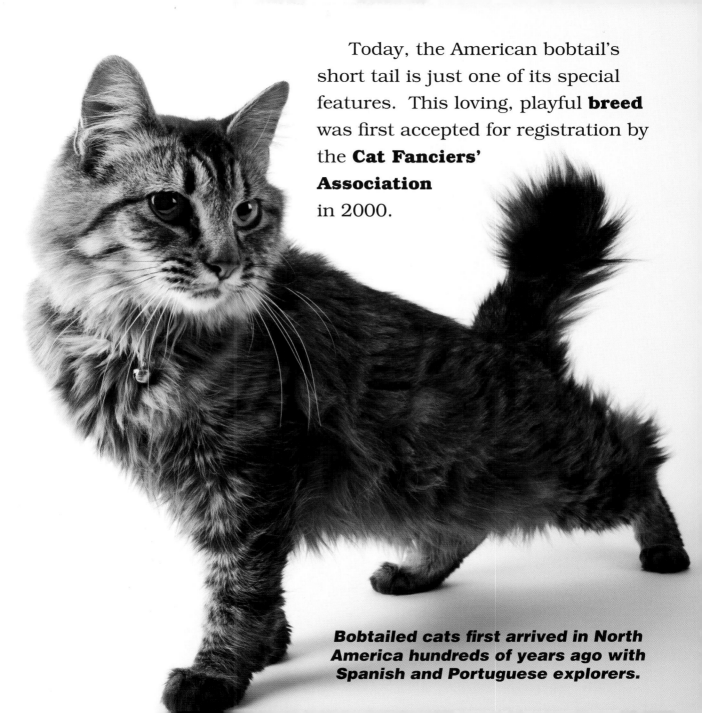

Today, the American bobtail's short tail is just one of its special features. This loving, playful **breed** was first accepted for registration by the **Cat Fanciers' Association** in 2000.

Bobtailed cats first arrived in North America hundreds of years ago with Spanish and Portuguese explorers.

QUALITIES

Some people believe the American bobtail descends from a wild bobcat. They certainly look wild! But these **domestic** cats are lively without being overly active. They are clownish and love to play. They'll even learn to play fetch! In fact, some owners say their bobtails are like dogs.

Most American bobtails are highly social. They love the entire family rather than just one person. In addition, this **breed** gets along with small children and even the family dog.

American bobtail cats are also very smart. Bobtails have the mysterious ability to free themselves from locked cages and rooms. Owners catch them standing on their hind legs, using their front paws to turn doorknobs!

American bobtails travel well, so they are popular companions for truck drivers.

COAT AND COLOR

These well-behaved cats come in many colors. Some American bobtails are the usual colors of black, brown, cream, or white. Others range from red to blue to lavender!

In addition to their wide range of colors, bobtails have a large variety of coat patterns. For example, some have a spotted coat pattern. Others have stripes. Still others have both!

American bobtail cats may have short or long hair. The short-haired bobtail's coat is soft and plush. The long-haired bobtail has medium to long hair, but the coat resists **matting**.

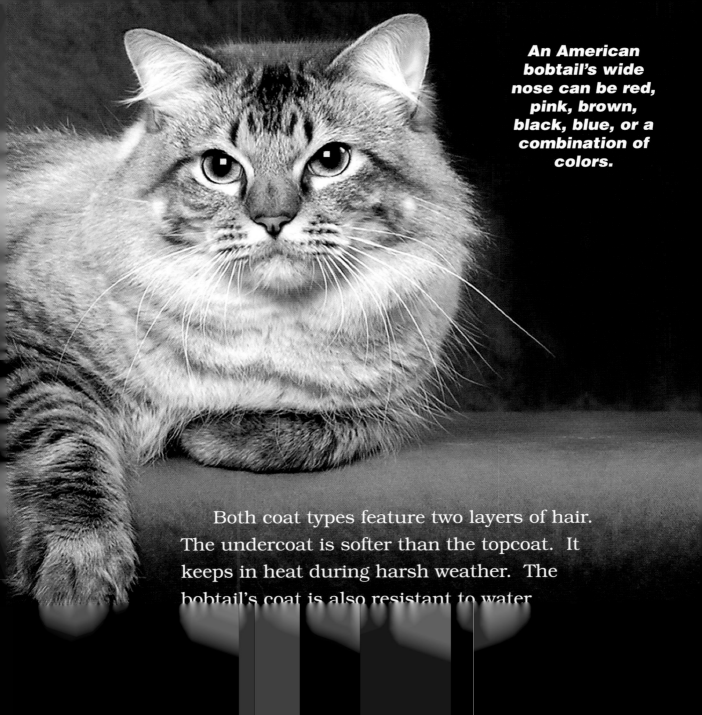

An American bobtail's wide nose can be red, pink, brown, black, blue, or a combination of colors.

Both coat types feature two layers of hair. The undercoat is softer than the topcoat. It keeps in heat during harsh weather. The bobtail's coat is also resistant to water.

SIZE

It's easy to see why people believe American bobtails come from wild ancestors. These cats are big and muscular. Their powerful, athletic bodies are moderately long. With all that muscle, males weigh between 12 and 16 pounds (5.4 and 7.3 kg). Females weigh 7 to 11 pounds (3.2 to 5.0 kg).

The American bobtail rests on large, round paws. This stocky cat has a large chest and wide hips. Its broad head features full cheeks and a wide forehead. Furry ears and large, almond-shaped eyes complete the look.

Even these impressive features won't distract you from this **breed**'s tail! The stubby tail is passed down from older generations. It is usually one to four inches (2.5 to 10 cm) long. The tail may be straight, curved, bumpy, or knotted. No two are exactly alike!

The bobtail's rear legs are longer than its front legs. So, its straight back sits at a slant.

CARE

American bobtail cats are a strong, healthy **breed**. They do not have any special health issues. Of course, proper care is a key part of keeping American bobtails healthy.

Like all cats, this breed requires regular **vaccines** and yearly visits to the veterinarian. At these visits, the veterinarian will check your cat's eyes, ears, nose, teeth, tummy, and more. If breeding is not desired, the veterinarian can **spay** or **neuter** your cat as well.

If you want a cat that doesn't require much grooming, an American bobtail could be the breed for you. Whether long-haired or short-haired, these cats need little brushing. Both types require only occasional bathing.

All cats need monthly teeth cleaning. This prevents bacteria from growing and making your pet ill. Claw trimming and a scratching post are important, too. They will prevent ruined furniture and scratched skin.

Wise owners groom and bathe their cats from an early age to prevent battles later on!

FEEDING

Like all their feline cousins, American bobtail cats need a healthy diet. Just like you, they need a wide variety of **nutrients** including protein, carbohydrates, and fat. Vitamins and minerals are also essential for their health.

Luckily, quality cat food with all the necessary nutrients is easy to find. Veterinarians and pet and grocery stores stock many types.

Cat food comes in dry, semimoist, and moist varieties. Dry food helps clean teeth and does not spoil. Semimoist food can also be left out of the refrigerator. Yet some cats prefer moist food. Just be careful not to leave it out too long. The food may attract bugs or spoil and make your cat sick.

Water is also vital to the American bobtail's healthy diet. It helps with **digestion** and temperature control. So, provide clean water daily to keep your pet in top shape.

Cats are naturally meat eaters. But, they need to eat more than just meat to stay healthy.

KITTENS

American bobtails mature more slowly than other cat **breeds**. They take two to three years to fully develop. However, most cats are ready to reproduce by five months of age. So, **spay** or **neuter** cats at an early age if they will not be bred.

The American bobtail is **pregnant** for about 65 days. **Litters** of four kittens are most common. The mother stays close to her babies because they are completely helpless. Kittens cannot see, hear, or walk at birth.

After 10 to 12 long, dark days, kittens gain their senses. By 3 weeks, they can walk around and explore their world. They stay near their mother to nurse for several more weeks. By 12 weeks, American bobtail kittens are ready to be adopted.

Kittens learn how to play by spending time with one another.

BUYING A KITTEN

Good **breeders** never separate a kitten from its mother too early. They also know the kitten's parents and its health history. Therefore, buying an American bobtail from a reputable breeder is best. Good breeders want each kitten to find a happy home.

Before you bring home your American bobtail, you'll need some supplies. A **litter box** is very important! Many kittens have already learned to use one. A scratching post and grooming and dental tools are also wise to have on hand.

With good care and a loving home, the American bobtail cat will be with you for more than a decade. Healthy American bobtails can live 12 to 21 years! If you're ready for this commitment, you'll love having an entertaining American bobtail in your home.

A breed rescue is another place to look for a pet that needs a new home.

GLOSSARY

agile - able to move quickly or easily.

breed - a group of animals sharing the same ancestors and appearance. A breeder is a person who raises animals. Raising animals is often called breeding them.

Cat Fanciers' Association - a group that sets the standards for judging all breeds of cats.

digestion - the process of breaking down food into simpler substances the body can absorb.

domestic - tame, especially relating to animals.

Felidae (FEHL-uh-dee) - the scientific Latin name for the cat family. Members of this family are called felids. They include lions, tigers, leopards, jaguars, cougars, wildcats, lynx, cheetahs, and domestic cats.

litter - all of the kittens born at one time to a mother cat.

litter box - a box filled with cat litter, which is similar to sand. Cats use litter boxes to bury their waste.

matting - forming into a tangled mass.

neuter (NOO-tuhr) - to remove a male animal's reproductive glands.

nutrient - a substance found in food and used in the body. It promotes growth, maintenance, and repair.

pregnant - having one or more babies growing within the body.

sanctuary - a place that provides shelter or safety for wildlife.

spay - to remove a female animal's reproductive organs.

tabby - a coat pattern featuring stripes or splotches of a dark color on a lighter background. Individual hairs are banded with light and dark colors.

vaccine (vak-SEEN) - a shot given to prevent illness or disease.

WEB SITES

To learn more about American bobtail cats, visit ABDO Publishing Company online. Web sites about American bobtail cats are featured on our Book Links page. These links are routinely monitored and updated to provide the most current information available.

www.abdopublishing.com

INDEX